WAKEFIELD & DISTRICT

THROUGH TIME

Peter Tuffrey

Best wishes

from

Peter Tuffrey

AMBERLEY PUBLISHING

First published 2015

Amberley Publishing
The Hill, Stroud
Gloucestershire, GL5 4EP

www.amberley-books.com

Copyright © Peter Tuffrey, 2015

The right of Peter Tuffrey to be identified as the
Author of this work has been asserted in accordance
with the Copyrights, Designs and Patents Act 1988.

ISBN 978 1 4456 4639 8 (print)
ISBN 978 1 4456 4640 4 (ebook)

British Library Cataloguing in Publication Data.
A catalogue record for this book is available from
the British Library.

Typesetting by Amberley Publishing.
Printed in the UK.

Introduction

In this book, many of the old photographs used for comparison with modern ones fall largely into the period of 1905–35. They were taken by the armies of postcard photographers that flourished during this period, capturing virtually any scene they considered necessary to make a saleable product. They were using the relatively new art of photography, not to mention postcards – a novel and new form of communication. For their efforts we are grateful, as they have made a unique and invaluable record of the city and a number of the outlying districts are covered here.

To look at Wakefield through time, I have chosen mainly the old city areas that were favourites of the postcard photographers and these included, among others: The Bull Ring, Westgate, Kirkgate, Upper Kirkgate, Northgate and Westgate End. During the early twentieth century, Wakefield's buildings were a mixture of Georgian, Victorian and quite a number of buildings dated from the sixteenth century or even earlier.

The period also marked a time for a major rethink of the city's transport systems to outlying areas. Although it could be said they were served well by steam locomotives, trundling here and there and stopping at quaint wayside stations, it was considered a good commercial proposition to introduce electric tramways. Consequently, both open- and covered-top vehicles are seen in the old pictures weaving in and out of the city's slim streets.

Obviously, new buildings continued to be erected throughout the Edwardian period and later, and motorised buses eventually superseded the tramways. Additionally, slum clearance began in earnest in the 1920s and '30s with the development of council housing. However, after the Second World War, and the passing of the Town and County Planning Act in 1947, the city had some big decisions to make, as did many other British towns and cities. Many produced development plans in the 1950s and these were executed largely during the 1960s. Inevitably, this meant city and town centres were rationalised with business, shopping and residential zones clearly defined. Naturally, all of this had to work in unison with a motorised traffic system that could bring traffic successfully in and out of central areas as well as take passing traffic around instead of through them.

In carrying out redevelopment, Wakefield Council in the post-war years authorised the demolition of a number of Georgian buildings as well as many mid-to-late nineteenth-century properties. In their place sprang up high-rise flats, commercial and civic buildings that can loosely be described as Brutalist in style. It cannot be argued that some nineteenth-century properties with poor sanitation and amenities did not deserve to meet the demolition men and that living standards and the flow of traffic has not been vastly improved.

However, in the 1970s, the council (very wisely, it has to be said) started to take stock of itself, even though some may argue that this had come a little too late with regard to the number of buildings demolished and the new ones erected. Throughout the decade, the council readily accepted its rich heritage and designated certain parts of the city as conservation areas. After Wakefield became a Metropolitan district in 1974, certain districts of outlying towns and villages were also designated in the same way. It is interesting to note that great thought went into all this and how it might be maintained, with a number documents produced to be accessed and understood by residents and developers alike.

From time to time, all of the decisions regarding conservation areas have been updated and documents produced that are easily accessed online. On reading many of the conservation area documents, it is quite alarming to discover that many of the buildings erected during the 1960s are now considered to be grossly unattractive and not worthy of the slightest consideration for listing status. That aside, the recent imaginative regeneration of the tower block flats in the city centre has won national awards and have made for an interesting discussion on their contribution to Wakefield's impressive skyline.

During the last few years, several major projects have been completed, including the resiting of Westgate station; the establishment of Wakefield One to include council offices, the museum and library; and the building of the Hepworth Wakefield. This latter not only includes the celebration of sculptress Barbara Hepthworth's work in the first purpose-built gallery for decades, but also gives more display space to art works transferred from the small, once highly regarded Wentworth Terrace Art Gallery.

At the time of writing there are other major projects being undertaken by the council itself or in conjunction with other parties. These include the renovation of Wakefield Kirkgate railway station as well as the lower Kirkgate area itself; the establishment of a Civic Quarter, which will embrace some of the city's most impressive buildings including the court house, town hall and police station.

With great thought, undertaken from the 1970s, Wakefield, albeit a small city, has slowly been putting its house in order on many levels. For my part, it has been extremely rewarding and enlightening to research and illustrate *Wakefield & District Through Time*.

Acknowledgements

I would like to thank the following people for their help: Norman Ellis, Kevin Grundy, Phillip Grundy. Special thanks are due to my son Tristram Tuffrey for his general help and advice. Kate Taylor kindly read through the final manuscript.

Albion Street, North Side

Looking from Leeds Road towards College Grove Road, the north side of Albion Street, existing to the north of the city centre, is featured here. The street line has changed a little; the group of central buildings remain, but much redevelopment during the intervening period at the street's western and eastern points can be detected. Remarkably, the small perimeter walls on the group of central properties survive, though there are details missing from the top of the attic windows. Further down, classical-style doorways and window embellishments survive on an otherwise run-down property. Predictably, perhaps, all the windows in the houses have been changed. In the modern picture, to the left, are the backs of the newish buildings for the Queen Elizabeth Grammar School and have their fronts facing the school grounds. In the old picture a Midland Railway Co. poster advertises a direct route from Wakefield to the west of England, and a service between Wakefield and Barnsley.

Alverthorpe Road

Alverthorpe Road extends north from Dewsbury Road to a T-junction with Batley Road and Balne Lane. Early examples of housing along Alverthorpe Road mainly show pockets of small terraced dwellings. But throughout the twentieth century and into the present one, a variety of properties have been erected. The stretch of two-storey terraced properties, with attic skylights on the east side of the thoroughfare, appear to have undergone cosmetic rather than dramatic structural modifications, their gardens still neatly bordered by low brick walls. These cosmetic, and largely expected, alterations include window and door replacements to the more durable and practical double-glazed variety. Gone, however, are the days of traders with horse-drawn drays touring local districts selling a wide range of goods, as may be seen occurring in the top picture. Gone too, for the most part, are the times when young children could safely play in the road. Along Alverthorpe Road, some small shops thrive, as they once did quite nicely in former times. There is even a fish-and-chip shop.

Ashleigh Avenue

Extending north from Dewsbury Road, Ashleigh Avenue, according to Kate Taylor in *Not So Merry Wakefield* (2005), was part of the land originally developed in 1908 and laid out in parallel avenues as the Garden City. 'The scheme reflected the idealism of a group of Quakers ... who wanted to provide cheap plots of land where working people could build their own homes and enjoy their own gardens,' said the author. But, she points out, plots in Ashleigh Avenue remained vacant until the 1930s. Builder George Crook then acquired and developed all the remaining sites, erecting on them identical semi-detached properties for rent. Obviously, the rows of trees, mere saplings in the top picture, have grown considerably and add to the pleasant character of the thoroughfare. A slight criticism might be made concerning the design of the properties added to form a crescent at the end of the avenue. While out of keeping, they are, nonetheless, well kept.

Blenheim Road

Blenheim Road, stretching from Leeds Road and merging with Richmond Road, has been captured by a postcard photographer pointing his camera in a north-easterly direction. To the right he has portrayed a large Dutch-gabled property on the southern side of the street, along with a number of individuals going about their daily business. One of the road's large villas became Wakefield Council's first maternity hospital. While there are pockets of interesting housing developments here, this has been spoiled over the years by insensitive infilling of properties of all sizes and descriptions and is probably why the road does not fall into Wakefield's St John's Conservation Area. Nonetheless, it still retains its former leafy, exclusive air of the early twentieth century and is still one of Wakefield's most desirable areas in which professionals choose to live.

MECHANICS INSTITUTE, TOWN HALL
AND COUNTY HALL, WAKEFIELD.

Bond Street/Cliff Parade, County Hall

To house the headquarters of the West Riding County Council (WRCC), formed in 1889, tenders were invited three years later for the design of a suitable building. James Gibson and Samuel Russell's drawing, said to be 'of an Art nouveau character with Italian qualities to the decorations', was accepted and the building erected at the corner of Bond Street and Cliff Parade between 1894 and 1898. It was opened by the chairman of the WRCC on 22 February 1898. Grindleford stone ashlar was used on the exterior, which was richly carved by W. Birnie of Edinburgh. George Crook of Wakefield added new wings to the building between 1912 and 1915. The WRCC occupied the premises until the organisation was abolished in 1974. The building was inherited by the newly established West Yorkshire County Council until, in turn, it was abolished in 1986. Shortly afterwards, the county hall was acquired by the City of Wakefield Metropolitan District Council, formed in 1974.

Bond Street, The Towers

Stretching north–south, between Bell Street and the Wentworth Street/Wentworth Terrace junction, Bond Street is depicted facing north. The former Wakefield Art Gallery is just visible in the distance. Sadly the building on the left has since been demolished to accommodate Wakefield College and one of the pinnacles on a terrace known as the Towers (Nos 20, 22, 24, 26, 28) is presently missing from the property's southern corner. The Gothic, red-brick, three-storey terrace, with canted projecting bays, dates from the late nineteenth century and, although mainly used for offices today, continues to add character to the street. Several buildings on the east side and to the south, though out of view, are Grade II listed. Others, Nos 20 to 44, are locally listed buildings. There is an argument that the out of scale buildings on the street's west side spoil the view of the early and later nineteenth-century ones on the opposite side. Alternatively, there is a case that all this makes for an interesting and visually exciting streetscape, which is part of the Wentworth Terrace Conservation Area.

Bradford Road

This section of Bradford Road is on the stretch between Wrenthorpe Road/Red Hall Lane junction and Leeds Road. In the top picture, a youth is perched on a seat alongside a milk churn in a low, open-backed horse-drawn cart. While delivering milk by this method may seem primitive and even unhygienic to us now, the practice of delivering produce to our doorsteps has even been adopted by many large supermarkets today. Once a mere cart track, Bradford Road, like countless others up and down the country, has been transformed to conform with present-day standards, especially with the provision of lanes for cyclists. Noticeable too is the change from old gas lamps to modern electric lighting. Along the section visible, there has been some infilling of properties, yet the open land to the rear is currently much overgrown. Just beyond the bend is the Bay Horse public house which, as part of its services, currently delivers curries or Sunday lunches.

Bread Street

The top picture of Bread Street, in the 1920s and facing south, was taken by Doncaster-based photographer Edgar Leonard Scrivens. The street forms part of the Wakefield Cathedral Conservation Area, designated in 1975. The former Tetley house, the Mitre, existing here 1739–1960, is at the end of the properties on the left with the cathedral in the distance. On the left is No. 26 Bread Street, the rear of No. 19 Cross Square – the three-storey, late-eighteenth-century building that was, much later, converted to the Black Rock public house (also known as the New Inn). No. 26 is a Grade II listed building, along with a number of other properties in the thoroughfare, that date from the late eighteenth and early nineteenth centuries. At the time of the top picture, C. A. Cutts was the licensed victualler of the Black Rock. Unfortunately, movement through the street's southern end is now partially restricted by an unsightly 1960s brick extension. The quaint view towards the cathedral has been spoilt by this intrusion, and large wheelie bins also add to the malaise.

Brook Street, John Dudding, Fruit and Potato Merchant

Present Dudding family members state that fruit and potato merchant J. Dudding is pictured in the straw boater at his business premises, seen in the top picture, at No. 37 Brook Street, facing west. His wife and two daughters, May and Agatha, are also included in the picture. The firm left this site during the late 1960s and moved to Jacobs Well Lane, but after a large fire in 2004, settled in Belle Vue. During the period separating the two pictures, the old Dudding site appears to have been redeveloped and renumbered 37 and 37A. *Wakefield Historical Society's Guide to Selected Historical Buildings in Wakefield* informs Brook Street was once known as Goodybower and is mentioned in the medieval Wakefield Cycle of Mystery plays. A strong interest in exotic and extraordinary pets, developed over the last few decades, is reflected in the Aquatica store depicted in the modern picture, announcing the sale of 'snakes, lizards and rats'.

Bull Ring and Queen Victoria Statue

Financed through public subscription, the heroic-size bronze statue of Queen Victoria was unveiled by The Mayoress Mrs H. S. Childe in the Bull Ring on 15 February 1905. Francis John Williamson was the sculptor and it was cast by A. B. Burton of the Thames Ditton bronze foundry in Surrey. An inscription on the work states, 'This statue was erected by the citizens of Wakefield as a memorial to their great and good Queen.' The statue is based on Williamson's marble statue of Victoria, sculpted in 1887 at the time of her Golden Jubilee. Forty-five years after the unveiling, the monument was removed to Denby Dale Road at the entrance to Clarence Park. However, it was returned to its original position in 1985 only to be removed once again during October 2009 to a new home in Castrop Rauxel Square in Wakefield's civic quarter, outside county hall. The bronze has a Grade II listing.

Bull Ring/Cross Square Junction

The wedge-shaped, ashlar, four-storey building at the Bull Ring/Cross Square corner was designed by Leeds architect Percy Robinson (1868–1950), who is also noted for his impressive commercial premises in that city as well as a number of buildings in other parts of the country. The Wakefield building was erected in 1906 in the classical style with a canted façade and domed cupola. Although out of scale and different in style and materials to other buildings in Cross Street, it is a striking building nonetheless. Numerous businesses have occupied the building throughout its existence, but in 2014, Wakefield Civic Society's Design Awards gave formal recognition to the present Café Marmalade frontage. The judges felt that the owners had given this corner a real lift. However, it is curious that in both the old and new pictures there are 'To Let' signs in the lower and upper floors, suggesting that the landmark building, impressive as its appearance may be, struggles to be fully occupied long term.

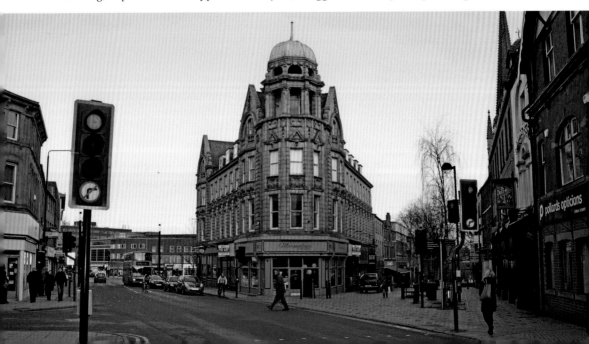

Bull Ring, Facing North with Tram for Leeds

A comparison of the old and new pictures taken on the east side of the Bull Ring, facing north along Northgate, reveals how far this side has been set back and the corners rounded at the Union Street junction. It is disappointing that the modern picture reveals the Bull Ring, at the heart of Wakefield city centre and steeped in history, currently has no real buildings of character or with any long history. That aside, in the old view, the conductor in the Yorkshire (West Riding) Electric Tramways Co. Ltd's car No. 5 waits patiently for departure time to Leeds. Meanwhile, the driver of approaching car No. 15 threads his way through the vicinity carefully, anticipating pedestrians dashing across while making his way south to Sandal. The only easily recognisable building to survive the passage of time is the Talbot & Falcon public house on the right, dating from *c.* 1700 and rebuilt in 1928.

Bull Ring, Jackson's Store/Vegas Bar

Jackson's store, occupying part of the Percy Robinson-designed building at the Bull Ring/ Cross Street junction, is pictured above facing the Bull Ring. Staff and a boy are proudly posing outside the premises, and advertisements on the building itself and within the window displays announce the sale of ladies' and gents' boots, shoes and hats. The window displays also exhibit a fine array of straw boaters and coats. The modern picture shows how technology, social trends and commercial advertising have altered over the intervening years. The Vegas Bar, with a frontage struggling to be in tune with the rest of the building, offers a wide variety of drinks along with Sky Sports entertainment and WiFi for customers. They can also access information about the venue on Facebook. While there is a harmony with the building in the way Jackson's advertise their products, the council's Cathedral Conservation Area report states commercial frontages in the vicinity could benefit from improvement and the removal of large fascia boards, which detract from the appearance of a number of prominent properties.

Bull Ring, Looking South to Westmorland Street

Once a hive of activity with pedestrians, trams and ramshackle early motorbuses criss-crossing in all directions over the Bull Ring, Queen Victoria almost appears to be mildly amused. Many of the three-storey buildings in the older view have presence, design uniformity and character, such as the Griffin Hotel, Maypole Dairy, Hague Bros buildings and Bradleys (*right*). Overall, the impression of the buildings in the modern view is bleak and shouts disharmony, functional as they may be. Nevertheless, with regard to the desolate Bull Ring open space, the council has recognised it is underused and featureless; they plan improvements for a more inviting and attractive environment to encourage people to use the area.

Bull Ring, Northgate/Union Street North Corner

Although these two pictures do not match up identically, they illustrate quite adequately how the corner has been drastically altered. In the top picture, the corner property provided business premises for baker and confectioner Charles Hagenbach (of Swiss Ancestry) for a number of years. To the left was the Old Crown Yard, which led to the company's bakery. Similar views to this one, showing traders posing, sometimes with family, staff, horse and drays, or early motor vehicles, were taken by armies of photographers to produce postcard views. That practice seemed to be the fashion during the early twentieth century but is rarely seen today. As Hagenbach's business expanded, shops were established in other Wakefield district areas and vehicles like the ones seen here were used to make deliveries. After the Second World War, this corner was realigned and the business moved elsewhere in the city, establishing a bakery in Chald Lane and shops in Little Westgate and the Springs. In time, Hagenbach's was one of Yorkshire's biggest bakery businesses, with nearly forty shops and restaurants in the county, but in 1957, it was sold to Allied Bakeries.

Bull Ring, Northgate/Union Street South Corner

The top picture illustrates the Bull Ring's Northgate/Union Street south corner (adjoining properties on the area's east side) before alterations. Although looking a little ramshackle, we might speculate about whether the decision to demolish all the buildings would have been taken today. Part of the reason for setting back the corner and redeveloping much of the east side must have been to facilitate the easy flow of motor vehicle traffic in and around the area and to bring the retail outlets up to modern standards. But presently, this side of the Bull Ring is no longer part of a major traffic route and has no architectural merit, according to the Council's Cathedral Conservation Area report: 'There are no buildings included on the local list on Bull Ring ... and none considered worthy of inclusion,' the document states.

Bull Ring, Strafford Arms

The sheer size of the original Strafford Arms, dating from *c.* 1725 and built on the site of the Old Black Swan, is most impressive as can be seen from the top view looking north-east. It obviously needed to be this size because, for many years, it was Wakefield's principal coaching inn, the city being a major centre for travel to London. The Strafford Arms was also the chief posting-house and from here ran the Royal Mail to Leeds, London, Manchester, York and Sheffield. Many tired and weary travellers would break their long, arduous journeys in the town so a large army of staff at the Strafford Arms would be employed to cater for their every need. While lamenting the demise of the marvellous building itself, clearly its original function has vastly changed over the years. No more is there a need to cater for 'coaching' travellers or to have a building of such a vast size. It was rebuilt in 1876, modernised in 1967 and rebuilt once more in 1980. Today, despite its uninspiring appearance, the building is much more in tune with today's requirements. It is a popular public house with a sizeable function room, frequently used for a variety of events.

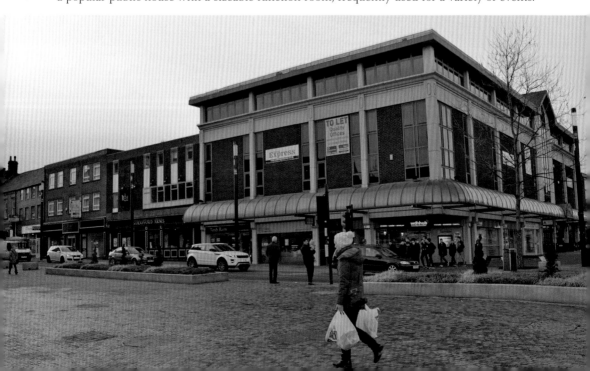

Cliff Lane Looking South

Both views show Cliff Lane facing south from Burton Street to Cliff Parade. While revealing that vast changes have occurred on each side, there is perhaps only a slight alteration to the thoroughfare's width and course. At the time of the top picture, to the left, among the group of buildings, was the West Riding Depot, while out of view to the right would be, perhaps, the tip of Cliff Field House gardens and the cattle pens at Westgate railway station. In the distance, the tall, curious, slim building, still visible today, at No. 1 Back Lane, was occupied by the Roundabout Tavern, dating back to 1837 but subsequently titled the Priory. Cliff Lane presently forms part of Merchant Gate, where Wakefield's new colossal flagship building on the left, Wakefield One, opened to the public on Monday 29 October 2012. The building offers customers across the district one point of contact for a range of council services. There is also a new library in the building and a museum located on the lower ground floor. The Merchant Gate scheme comprises a 17-acre site in Wakefield's commercial quarter.

Cross Square, Facing South East

Changes in how motor vehicles access and move around the city centre, as well as park within its streets, have resulted in Cross Square becoming a pedestrianised, paved area. This occurred during the early 1990s after the refurbishment of the cathedral precinct began. Cross Square takes its name from the market cross, formerly situated at its western end. It has also become part of the Wakefield Cathedral Conservation Area. The thoroughfare still fulfils the same function as it has done for many years – providing a number of unique retail outlets for Wakefield shoppers. Once well-known premises may be seen on the right in the top picture, including Webster Brothers' shop and café, Dyson's jewellers, and M. I. Eggleston's ladies' outfitting store. A number of the street's buildings survive from the time of the earlier picture and originally date from the late eighteenth and nineteenth centuries. The ugly 1960s structures arguably spoil the street's overall appearance.

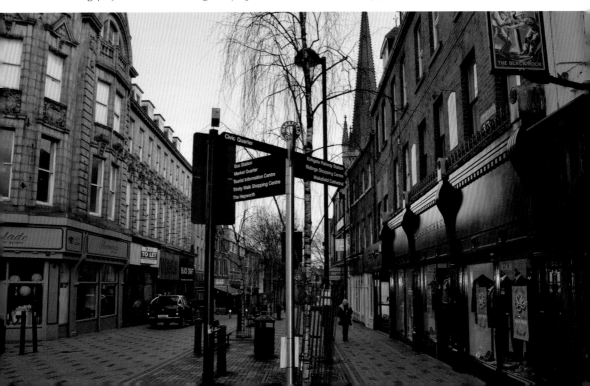

Denby Dale Road, Facing North

This short, narrow stretch of Denby Dale Road presently extends from the Charlesworth Way/ Denby Dale roundabout to the one on Ings Road. The view is looking north. In the top picture, adjacent to the bridge, is a signal box close to the West Riding junction where the lines of the Bradford, Wakefield & Leeds Line once met with those of the West Riding & Grimsby's. Quite noticeably, the most dramatic changes have occurred on either side of the road, with all the buildings being demolished, including Dale Street, which once extended off to the right. The retail developments on each side reflect the changes over the last fifty years or more in the way we buy goods, no matter how large or small. A vast increase in the size of retail outlets is also perceived.

Drury Lane, Carnegie Library

Scottish-American industrialist Andrew Carnegie (1835–1919), with a massive personal fortune, gave a large amount away for the establishment of 660 libraries in the UK. Wakefield's Mayor, Henry S. Childe, successfully secured £8,000 from the philanthropic Carnegie for the building of a library in the city. This was on condition that the Public Library Act (1850) was activated, allowing the levying of a penny rate. Wakefield's Carnegie Library was designed by Messrs Trimmell, Cox & Davison and built by Messrs Bagnall Bros. Local man Charles Skidmore donated 2,000 books in a ceremony where Andrew Carnegie formally opened the new library on 20 June 1906. The building ceased to be used as a library in 2012, when the activity was transferred to a new civic building – Wakefield One. The Grade II listed building is currently being extensively refurbished by the Art House. Situated directly adjacent to the existing Art House building that was completed in the Phase 1 development, the old library building will open in spring 2015. The facility will provide rentable artists' studios, multi-use spaces, learning areas and permanent linkage to the existing Art House building. The Art House was established in 1994 by a group of artists in response to the lack of facilities and opportunities for disabled artists in the visual arts and crafts. Phase One was completed in 2008, providing an accessible building encompassing fourteen managed studios and workshop spaces in Wakefield city centre. Wakefield Council's ten-year renaissance strategy for the city focuses on the arts as one of the drivers for regeneration.

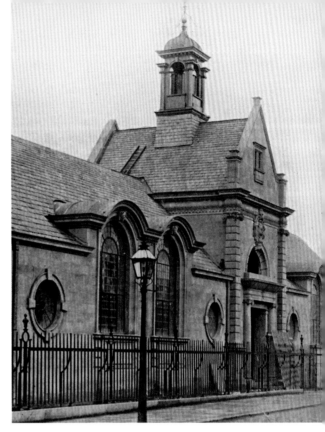

athing new life in to the Old Library
34 artists' studios, public spaces and more...

Howard Street

Howard Street is depicted facing east from Northgate, where quite drastic changes are apparent. At the time of the top picture, *c.* 1910, Howard Street, once called Chestnut Lane, was made up of lower middle-class housing, built from around 1830 onwards. The thoroughfare extended to Savile Street and beyond was Hatfield Street. It is now truncated and much of the former area has been redeveloped, becoming part of a pleasant arrangement of new properties – Hatfield Court Sheltered Housing. The pub on the corner, currently titled The College, has also passed through a number of owners and seen a fair amount of physical change. Dating from at least 1840, with Jessie Wilcock as licensee, it was formerly titled The Chestnut Tree and started life as a beerhouse. Previous owners have included the Fernandes Brewery, Mansfield Brewery and Wolverhampton-Dudley Breweries. At some point during the period separating the two pictures, it has undergone a makeover and emerged with what is known as a 'Brewers' Tudor' appearance.

Ings Lane/George Street, Cattle Market

A modern view to compare with the one in the top picture can only be obtained by sneaking into the Wakefield Royal Mail Sorting Office yard and pointing a camera towards George Street. However, I was welcomed there and even given a high-vis vest to wear while taking the modern picture. Dominating the top photograph, Wakefield cattle market, dating from 1765, formerly had a reputation as being one of the largest in the north of England. In 1835, it was recorded that 170,000 sheep and 13,500 cattle were sold here. A market was held on a fortnightly basis until 1849, when it continued as weekly event. Wakefield Corporation took control in 1938 but closure came in 1963. On George Street, the Cattle Market Hotel operated between 1887 and 1930, and the building survives. Adjacent is the Baptist chapel, in existence from 1844 but currently occupied by the New Life Christian Centre. Further along George Street, the Bull Fairhouse and Graziers are also extant.

Jacobs Well Lane

In the top picture, S. Raven, provision dealer, proudly announces the sale of Hovis Bread, Cadbury's Cocoa and Fry's Chocolate, among a number of other items, from a corner store in Jacob's Well Lane on the outskirts of the city. The premises also accommodates the Jacob's Well Lane Post Office. Judging by the number of children pictured outside the building, it was probably an old-style corner shop, popular and convenient to many folk living in the neighbourhood. The conversion of the premises to an Indian restaurant/takeaway does not necessarily imply that corner shops have disappeared from the area. In fact, several exist within a 100-yard radius. The building's change of use (Islamabad's has been catering for the needs of Wakefield diners for more than twenty years) shows how different and varied our eating habits have become over the last fifty years or more. It also shows how successfully other cultures and habits have blended into the English way of life and, for that, our lives are more enriched.

KIRKGATE BRIDGE AND CHANTRY, WAKEFIELD   928 / 8

Kirkgate, Chantry Bridge and Tram

A comparison of both pictures, looking north-east, reveals that the city's Chantry Bridge area was once a hive of activity, but this has since fallen away and it is now an idyllic backwater. The bridge, with sections dating from *c.* 1342, once provided a crossing over the River Calder for a main arterial road stretching from the Midlands and up through the town to Leeds. To gain an idea of how busy the narrow bridge was in 1901, a survey taken between Wednesday 1 May and Saturday 4 May recorded 5,304 horse-drawn vehicles, 8 traction engines, 15 motor cars, 3,530 bicycles and 629 horses and cattle. Before any proposal was submitted for trams to use the bridge, an inspection was made by a Board of Trade Inspector. Following authorisation, trams from the Yorkshire (West Riding) Electric Tramways Co. Ltd ran over the bridge from 1904. Among the many buildings in the background is the King's or Soke mill (immediately behind the tram), which was cleared in 1931 for the building of the new Wakefield Bridge to the west. This opened in 1933 and eventually took traffic away from the area. Currently, the old bridge has limited access for motor vehicles.

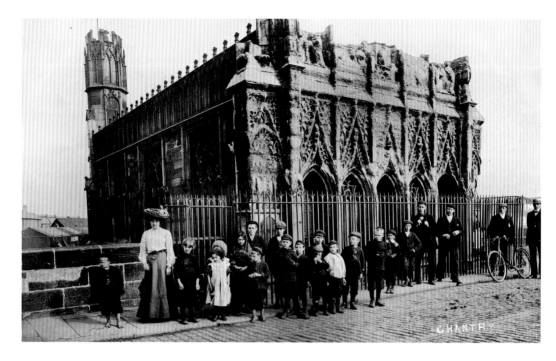

Kirkgate, Bridge Chapel

The chantry chapel of St Mary the Virgin dates from between 1342 and 1359. Following the 1547 Act for the Dissolution of the Chantries, it was acquired by Yorkshire's Savile family and, around 1568, was bequeathed to the Trustees of the Wakefield Poor. The chapel was transferred to the Church of England in 1842 and underwent restoration. The building reopened for worship in 1848 and eventually became a chapel of ease. A Friends of the Chapel was formed in 1990 and raised funds for building's repair and maintenance. Presently, it is under the authority of the Dean and Chapter of Wakefield Cathedral.

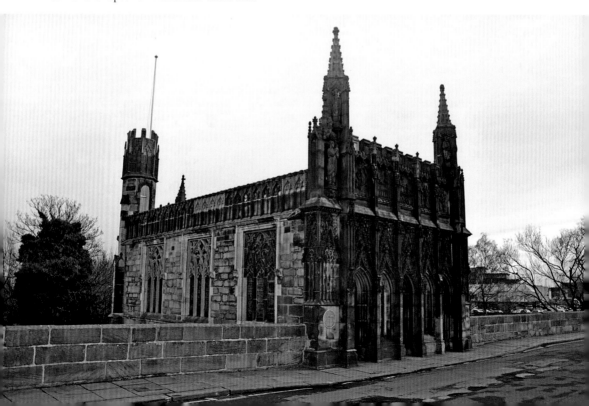

Kirkgate, Empire Cinema Site

The Empire, pictured above right, was designed by English theatrical architect Frank Matcham (1854–1920) as a variety theatre and opened on 20 December 1909. The building was owned by the Sherwood family, with films as well as theatrical performances being part of the entertainment programme. When the premises were taken over by Leeds firm the New Century Company, they were restyled Empire Super Cinema, the entertainment programme featuring films exclusively. From 1928, the building was in the hands of Gaumont and closure came on 30 July 1960. The site was subsequently cleared and redeveloped. Still existing (though much altered) is the building with the pointed gable, providing a good visual reference for a comparison of how the street line, as well as character, has been altered.

Kirkgate, Hargrave Bros.

Comment must be made about the superb design and craftsmanship that is evident on the shop frontage as well as the imaginative shop window illumination of the Hargrave Bros. ladies' clothes store at No. 164 Kirkgate. By comparison the modern store frontage, while adequate and informative, is merely functional. Are the two smartly dressed men shyly peeping through the downstairs windows in the picture the Hargrave brothers themselves? That has not been confirmed. In Hargrave's first-floor windows there are several notices: Dressmaking a Speciality, Mantle Show Rooms and Millinery Show Rooms. There are also two notices projecting from the building advertising a Perth Dye Works, all these suggesting the brothers offered a wide range of services for women. It may be argued that trading practices have changed considerably in this building over the years. Hargrave Bros. could rely on passing trade as well as word of mouth, people living in streets close by and newspaper advertisements for their business to flourish. That has become more difficult in this location today as there are fewer surrounding houses and limited opportunities for traffic to park outside the building. However, this has not deterred traders at the site, as there have been a number of different ones over the years. The company presently occupying all the floors in both Nos 164 and 162 has been there since the 1990s and has fully embraced modern trading practices; their website quite professionally gives the customer a virtual tour round the entire store.

Kirkgate, Looking North with Tram for Ossett

During the time separating top and bottom pictures, showing Kirkgate looking north, planning, with regard to building materials, street scale and design of buildings, appears to have gone wildly astray. However, an exciting streetscape certainly makes an interesting subject for discussion. Slightly to the left of the tram, the tall building – the Harewood Arms – was subsequently reduced in height and forms one of the only landmarks to place the two pictures in context and have any meaning for comparison. The curious three-gabled building, immediately to the right at the Kirkgate/Leigh Street corner, was titled six chimneys and is allegedly traceable to the Elizabethan period. After a partial collapse in 1941, the building was later demolished, but the name lives on in a Wetherspoon pub further north along the thoroughfare's east side. The cold presence of the structure covering much of the old Six Chimneys site may be loosely labelled Brutalist, and architecture of this type is arguably one of the most unpopular to pervade Britain's towns and cities.

Kirkgate, Looking South

Once again, the gabled building, the Harewood Arms (a Tetley house) in the centre of both pictures, facing east, gives them an anchor point. In the top picture, the encroachment of private and commercial motor vehicles has begun. There is also evidence that buildings along the thoroughfare are being torn apart to meet the insatiable needs of consumerism and entertainment. Looking at the bottom picture, all the buildings, moving south, beyond the one after the Harewood Arms, have been demolished and replaced. These include Blakeys, the Empire Theatre and the Crown & Anchor public house. Nearly all the properties on that side, moving north and out of view beyond the Harewood Arms, have been replaced. Additionally, on the west side, all the properties moving north from George Street to Upper Kirkgate were mostly replaced during the twentieth century's latter half. One common feature that has not changed during the intervening period (in fact, it has arguably got more garish and unsettling) is the commercial signage.

Kirkgate, Looking South

Shown here is a dramatically altered view of a narrow stretch of Kirkgate, facing south-west. In the old picture, the view is taken from around the Leigh Street area. Once noted streets and buildings have been swept away, including pubs and commercial premises on both sides, as the city struggled to come to grips with easing the flow of motorised traffic in and around the central area. The tall building still standing, just off-centre to the left in both pictures, has a date stone of 1905 and was formerly occupied by Lampen & Co., who had been there from at least 1857. Situated in the property adjacent was the King Edward VII public house.

Kirkgate New Bridge and Chantry Bridge

Wakefield Mayor Cllr Walter Emmett opened the city's new 75-foot-wide bridge across the River Calder on 1 June 1933, thus relieving the much older Chantry Bridge and Chapel of motorised traffic. At the same time, the Bishop of Wakefield, the Very Revd J. B. Seaton, blessed the new structure, which was built at a cost of around £78,000. The idea of the new bridge had been anticipated since the beginning of the twentieth century and Wakefield people might have argued its opening was well overdue. Road transport was already in the ascendancy during the 1930s. Between the wars, the number of private cars on Britain's roads had risen from 110,000 in 1919 to 2,034,000 in 1939; motorcycles from 115,000 to 488,000; buses, coaches and taxis from 44,000 to 90,000; and goods vehicles from 62,000 to 418,000. Already in 1939, people were spending around £135 million per year on private road transport. While the bridge may look quite calm around the time of its opening in the top picture, this is certainly not the case today, being an integral part of carrying traffic in and around the city.

Kirkgate, Old Ship Hotel

The Old Ship at No. 216 Kirkgate (formerly located to the left of the buildings in the modern picture) can be traced to at least 1818. Thomas Avison was noted as the landlord in 1834. Among the former owners of the pub were John Clayton, Joe Clayton, John Barrs and the Tadcaster Tower Brewery. The latter company was founded in 1882 and its name can be seen on a board above the Old Ship's frontage. At the time the picture was taken, Charles H. Salmon was the licensee and he is noted as being there between 1899–1906. The Tadcaster Tower Brewery was purchased by Hammonds Bradford Brewery Co. (later Hammonds United Breweries Limited) in 1946, and the last known landlady at the Old Ship was Maud Shea in 1964. Formerly existing to the right of the pub was Ship Yard and the King Edward Edward VII Inn (in Duchinak's premises). To the rear, and slightly west, was the Grove Iron Works and the Ings Foundry. Since the pub's demolition, a new spur from Ings Road to Kirkgate dominates much of the vacant area. Yet, the pub's name lives on, to the rear, in Ship Yard.

Kirkgate, Railway Station and Goods Yard

The Railway Clearing House Handbook of Railway Stations 1904 records that several companies had sidings in the goods yard at Kirkgate station. These included Brotherton & Co.'s Chemical and Cement Works, E. Green & Sons Ltd, Kilner & Son's Glass Bottle Works and Seamless Steel Boat Co. In the 1956 edition of the book, only the latter had ceased to maintain a place in the yard.

Kirkgate, Railway Station Interior, North Side
The station's overall roof and some platform buildings were removed in 1972 before Kirkgate was listed with Grade II status. A major scheme to restore the station commenced in August 2013 after many years of neglect. This £4.6-million project was driven by Groundwork Wakefield and multiple funding partners and will hopefully see the facilities brought back to life.

Kirkgate, Railway Station Exterior

The North Midland Railway completed the first Wakefield station, which was open for traffic from 5 October 1840. However, this was about 2 miles away from the town and was replaced and renamed Oakenshaw the following year, as the Manchester & Leeds Railway constructed extremely basic facilities in Kirkgate. The Great Northern Railway had attempted to build a line to Wakefield in the late 1840s, but the plans had been dismissed by Parliament, leaving the company to enter into an agreement with the Wakefield Pontefract & Goole Railway to run over their line to the town. The latter, with the M&L, formed the Lancashire & Yorkshire Railway and the company subsequently entered into an agreement with the GN to build a new station at Kirkgate. The task was completed in 1857 and the station was then managed by the L&Y.

Kirkgate, Regal Cinema

The Regal at the Sun Lane/Kirkgate corner was opened on 9 December 1935 by the Mayor of Wakefield, Alderman A. Charlesworth. The building was designed by Associated British Cinemas (ABC) architect William R. Glen and the first films shown were *Gold Diggers* and *Shanghai.* Seating was for 1,700 (1,100 in the stalls and 600 in the circle). Pop stars performed at the venue, which became known as the ABC in the 1960s, and among them were Helen Shapiro, Billy Fury, Adam Faith and the Beatles. After becoming part of the Cannon Cinemas chain in 1986, closure came in 1997. Like numerous old cinema buildings, the old Regal has struggled to find an alternative use.

Kirkgate, The Ridings Shopping Centre

The top picture was only taken in 1974, but the route past OObiDo has since become part of the Ridings Shopping Centre. Constructed in 1983, it comprises 110 units, including several restaurants and cafés. Many of the facilities and stores contained within the centre have gone some way to replace the straggling line of commercial properties that once made up much of Kirkgate's western side. The Ridings Centre was acquired by the Moorfield Group in November 2005 and underwent extensive refurbishment three years later, including three new entrances. Other incidental changes visible include the introduction, here and elsewhere in the UK, of free cash machines and the provision of parking facilities for cyclists. The fourteen-storey Brutalist Kirkgate blocks of flats (although not visible in the top picture) were built in 1969. They have survived against the odds and their recent refurbishment to an award-winning standard, with yellow cladding applied to the exterior, has divided opinion.

Kirkgate, with Agbrigg Tram

Drastic rationalisation has occurred here over the years, involving the removal of buildings to aid the implementation of a four-lane traffic flow system in and out of the city. Not only have the policeman and trams become redundant, but also the Crown Hotel, along with other properties on the left, and the Old King's Arms, to the right. The Crown, at No. 115 Ings Road, can trace its origins back to 1841 when Joseph Wainwright was landlord. The premises have also been titled Wainwright's Hotel, Kitson's Hotel and Dalby Hotel; the past owners include the Springwell Brewery, Leeds & Wakefield Brewery and Hammonds. Closure occurred in 1969, with Frank Dryden being the last tenant. On the opposite side, the Old King's Arms, at No. 241 Kirkgate, dates back to at least 1811 and was altered in 1893/94 to facilitate the widening of the railway bridge. Among the former owners were the Tadcaster Tower Brewery and closure occurred in 1927. Yorkshire (West Riding) Electric Tramways' car No. 9, heading for Agbrigg, entered service in 1904 as an open-top vehicle but, along with others, was fitted with a top cover *c.* 1911–14.

Kirkgate, with the Crown Hotel

Illustrated in the top picture, taken around 1905, is the Kirkgate/Ings Road junction showing the Crown Hotel and its impressive entrance, with columns and entablature. Yorkshire (West Riding) Electric Tramways' cars Nos 33 and 9, working the same Agbrigg to Thwaite Gate service but travelling in opposite directions, have met at this point. Dispensing chemist J. G. Hodgson's premises are to the left of the tram pole. All has now been swept away. The railway line, extending along the embankment and bridge, dominates the views. It leads to Kirkgate railway station, out of sight to the right, and is the only reminder of the once familiar older scene. The tall, robust, angled traffic light in the modern picture, arguably adds drama to the scene and underlines that the area is no longer a place for pedestrians to wander about in the road.

Kirkgate, with the Grey Horse Hotel

Fortunately, the Grey Horse pub is still in existence today, otherwise there may not be a clearly visibly landmark against which to match the two pictures. The pub can be traced to at least 1853 when Thomas Dobson was the licensee. Former owners have included Fernandes Brewery, John Smith's Brewery and Barnsley Oakwell Brewery. The view is looking to the junction of Kirkgate and Park Street, where the road takes a slight bend to the left before continuing northwards. The vast majority of properties have been demolished to facilitate the construction of a dual carriageway that leads to the Marsh Way ring road. Properties identified include the business premises of T. S. Perkin and C. Hodson's Kirkgate Meat Market. Dominating much of the modern view are the Kirkgate blocks of flats. Following recent refurbishment, roofs partially made of glass were installed. At night they are lit up and provide the Wakefield skyline with a spectacular sight.

Leeds Road, Fixing Overhead Tram Wires

Workers are pictured in Leeds Road, facing south, assembling overhead cables in readiness for the tram route from Sandal to Thwaite Gate, which was initially operated by the Wakefield & District Light Railway Co. The official opening of the route was on Monday 15 August 1904. From 1905, the tramway was run by the Yorkshire (West Riding) Electric Tramways Co. Ltd. The main contractor for the tramway was the Preston company of Dick, Kerr & Co. The company's horse-drawn tower wagon, along with their employees, leave a lot to be desired with regard to the strict health and safety procedures in operation today. Fortunately, at that time, Leeds Road was nowhere near as busy with motorised traffic as it is today, otherwise holding the horse steady for the convenience of the men working above, balancing on a strip of wood, may have proved difficult.

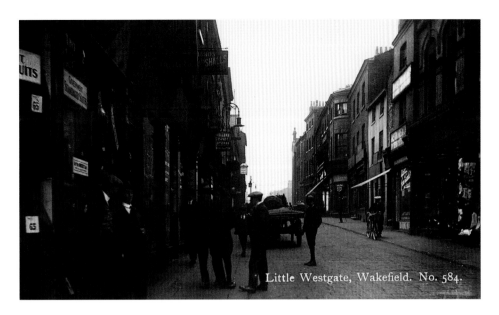

Little Westgate, Wakefield. No. 584.

Little Westgate

Postcard photographers regularly featured Wakefield's noted areas such as Westgate, Kirkgate and the Bull Ring, but few took pictures of the city's lesser-known streets like Little Westgate. It is also ironic that while few views exist of this street, Wakefield's noted photographers, George and John Hall, ran the Cathedral Studio from there, taking many popular views in and around the Wakefield area. Since the Hall brothers' time, Little Westgate has become part of the Cathedral Conservation Area, designated in 1975. It has been pedestrianised and some buildings have been listed Grade II, which is commendable. The Conservation Area report states 'there is little true architectural quality on the south side of the street,' which is lined with 1960s and '70s buildings. It could be argued that serious investment in small areas such as Little Westgate is perhaps restricted by the proliferation of shopping malls in and around the city centre.

Northgate, Bread Street and Cross Street

The top picture displays a fine array of individual shops accommodated in a group of buildings full of character. But, sweeping them away and replacing them with early 1960s box-like structures – as seen in the picture below – was badly timed. Only a few years later, the area became part of the Cathedral Conservation Area and the new buildings have courted heavy criticism. It is argued they are of no architectural merit or appropriate to their position and historic context opposite the Grade I listed cathedral. It is also added that they stand out too much because of their scale and massing and use of non-traditional materials.

Northgate, Clayton Hospital

Set in planted, landscaped grounds, the new Clayton Hospital and Wakefield General Dispensary opened in Northgate on 30 July 1879. It incorporated the Wakefield General Dispensary and the Wakefield House of Recovery and was supported by finance from former Wakefield Mayor Thomas Clayton, whose wealth had been derived from tallow chandlery. On his death in 1868, he left half his estate (approximately £600 annually) to the hospital. An extension to the building was opened in November 1900. It was financed by Mrs Louisa Milnes in memory of her husband Col Milnes Gaskell of Lupset Hall. By the mid-twentieth century, the building was known simply as Clayton Hospital. The hospital closed in 2012.

Northgate, Queen Elizabeth Grammar School

The Queen Elizabeth Grammar School was founded by Royal Charter of Queen Elizabeth in 1591 at the request of some of Wakefield's prominent people, who included Thomas Savile and his two sons. The original Elizabethan school building still exists on Brook Street. The school moved to the site depicted here in 1854 and into a building erected in 1833/34 to the designs of Manchester-based architect Richard Lane (1795–1880). Previously, the building was occupied by the West Riding Proprietary School. Today, the QEGS is still regarded as one of the country's best independent schools.

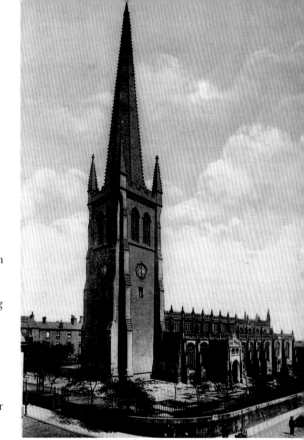

Northgate, Wakefield Cathedral

The splendid building, one of the finest in the city, occupies the site of an Anglo-Saxon church and preaching cross dedicated to All Hallows. Shortly after 1086, a Norman church was erected. Thereafter, the building was reconstructed and enlarged several times, notably in 1420 and later in the fifteenth century, until restoration was undertaken by Sir George Gilbert Scott and his son John Oldrid Scott between 1858 and 1874. Up to the sixteenth century, the church was known as All Hallows, and after the Reformation, All Saints. Wakefield's medieval parish church was elevated to the status of cathedral in 1888 when the Diocese of Wakefield was formed from the southern part of the Diocese of Ripon. In 2014, the Diocese was merged with the Dioceses of Bradford and Ripon/Leeds to become the Diocese of West Yorkshire and the Dales. This new diocese has the bizarre distinction of having two other cathedrals besides that of Wakefield. The cathedral's spire, standing at 247 feet, is the highest in Yorkshire, while the church itself forms the centrepiece of the Wakefield Cathedral Conservation Area, designated in 1975.

Pinderfields Road

The top picture of Pinderfields Road, facing south-west to what is now Marsh Way, was taken at a time (*c.* 1912) when it has often been said 'the world was still horse drawn'. Also, it may be stated that the appearance of a horse and dray along with men, who are probably from the council's street cleansing department, still raised more than a hint of curiosity from small children playing in the street. Since the coming of the motor car, this street has fallen in line with countless others; it has been laid with tarmac, planted with signage, double yellow lines have been applied at critical points and parking is restricted. A map of Wakefield (North) 1890 shows the three- and two-storey properties on the left along with other small pockets of housing; remaining areas on either side are shown as vacant open ground. Over the ensuing years, there has been significant infilling of properties along the road's entire stretch.

St John's North

Towards the end of the eighteenth century, local solicitor and developer John Lee was active in promoting a new town development on open land to the north and outside the Wakefield medieval town. St John's Square, completed around 1800, has on its north and west sides three-storey terraced town houses. Lee lived at No. 2 St John's Square; the property, facing east, had a substantial wooded and landscaped garden. His old property now carries a commemorative blue plaque. Under the leadership of Wakefield Civic Society, the square was extensively refurbished during the 1970s. St John's North, a stretch of three-storey properties, seen here looking from Leeds Road to St John's Square, was built just before the latter and to the east between 1791 and 1796. Unfortunately, this terrace is not matched by similar style buildings on the opposite side. Nos 2–24 are listed as Grade II*, but St John's North is described in the St John's Area Conservation report as 'little more than car parking area', adding that the line 'of cars parked against the terrace detracts rather from its appearance'.

St John's Square, St John's Church

The foundation stone for St John's church – Wakefield's first new post-Reformation church – was laid in 1791. The building was completed four years later. The design is attributed to Charles Watson (*c.* 1770–1836). During 1885, the church was altered and the tower rebuilt under the direction of London architect James Micklethwaite (1843–1906). A number of other alterations have since taken place. The early 1980s saw a reception room created at the rear of the church and, in 2007, a faculty was granted for a major internal redevelopment. St John's is designated at Grade II*.

Union Street and Bus Station

In a view taken from around the Union Street/Smallpage Yard junction, facing north-west to Northgate, the bus station's administration building dating from 1952 is on the left. The market hall covers the bus station's site, which has been relocated further to the east; the Northgate Court Apartments building (on the left) still surviving redevelopments in the area. It cannot be denied that the new bus station is much improved since the days of the old one, providing all the required comforts and up-to-date information for waiting passengers. Yet, the new market hall's existence on the old bus station site has not been without troubles. At the end of July 2014, Wakefield Council said the market had 'underperformed' and lost £193,000 a year since opening in 2008. Proposals to sell the land at Union Street to the owners of nearby Trinity Walk shopping centre were approved as a result at a cabinet meeting.

Upper Kirkgate, North Side

In contrast to the south side of Upper Kirkgate, the north side, depicted here, sits in the Cathedral Conservation Area and has several buildings that are listed: Nos 11–13 and 17–21. These include traditional building materials – red brick and stone flagged roofs. Nos 29–35 are locally listed structures. However, it is noticeable that a number of chimney pots are missing, there is unsightly stucco evident and some of the brickwork has been painted. Nevertheless, uniform building lines, along with a number of other features, has warranted the stretch worth of inclusion in the conservation area. Noted traders seen in the top picture include Maypole, Blaskey's, True-Form and the Northern Wines' stores. The Dog & Gun public house formerly existed on the eastern corner between 1802 and 1985. Thereafter, the building was demolished and the site redeveloped. Former owners included Beverley's and Wilson's Breweries.

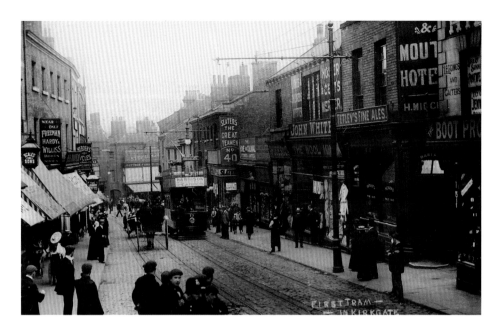

Upper Kirkgate, with the First Tram

The Yorkshire (West Riding) Electric Tramway ran cars along here from 1904 until 1934, and the cathedral precinct (out of view) was shortened to accommodate the lines. The first tram, a single-decker, is being watched by a fair number of excited spectators on 22 July 1904. The thoroughfare was widened in 1955 resulting in the demolition of many of the eighteenth- and nineteenth-century properties on the south side. This obliterated nearly all traces of the former medieval yards. Once well-known structures to disappear included the Bull & Mouth Hotel. New unattractive buildings were subsequently erected along the set back street line. The area is now considered to be a long square rather than a street, and significantly none of the south side buildings are included in the Cathedral Conservation Area. Presently, interspersed along the centre of the area are ornamental trees and various street furnishings.

Upper Kirkgate, with a Policeman on Traffic Duty

Directing traffic weaving in and out of the city's narrow streets, like Upper Kirkgate, is no longer a problem since the area was pedestrianised in 1975/76. In 1991/92, artist Tess Jaray redesigned the cathedral precinct, and among the alterations were replacement of the cathedral's south walls with York stone steps, repaving of the street and heavy stone planters constructed to support new lighting. During October/November 2006, to add street furnishing in front of the cathedral, low height plants in heavy stone planters were placed in a line along the street's central area. However, criticism has been made in the Cathedral Conservation Area report of the paving scheme, suggesting traditional paving materials, i.e. stone flags and setts, would have been more appropriate and in keeping with the stone-built cathedral.

Kirkgate Corner, Wakefield. No. 585.

Upper Kirkgate, with a Water and Scraper Car

When comparing old townscape views with modern ones, sometimes it is difficult to comprehend the changes that have taken place or comprehend a particular activity being undertaken. This may be true of the top picture, which captures the Yorkshire (West Riding) Electric Tramway Co.'s combined water and scraper car moving along Upper Kirkgate. The vehicle was built in 1904 by the Electric Railway & Tramway Carriage Works Ltd, Preston and contained a cylindrical water tank, surmounted by a roof carried on side stanchions. According to Pickles in *The Tramways of Dewsbury and Wakefield* (1980), the vehicle was based originally at Wakefield but transferred to Castleford and used for pre-opening test runs there. It was also used as a snow plough. Damaged in a fire at Castleford in 1917, it was later rebuilt as a permanent way car.

Warrengate, Looking North West to the Springs and Westmorland Street

The view north-west from Warrengate reveals, in a comparison of the two pictures, several significant alterations. The high wall to the right, beyond Vicarage Street, once enclosed, according to the OS Wakefield (North) 1890 map, Vicar's Croft Burial Ground and a bowling green. According to Ellis in *Bygone Wakefield & District* (1991), a watering place in the vicinity called the Waver became commonly known as the Springs and gave the street in the middle of the view its name. At one time, the Springs became one of the city's several bus terminals, witnessed by several vehicles in the top view, but this has been superseded. Westmorland Street, in the distance, was developed much later than the core area of the city and comprises three-storey terraced properties on the south side and 1930s and 1960s buildings on the opposite one. Several of the south side properties are listed and this section of the street, along with a short stretch of buildings on the same side, in the Springs, fall into the Cathedral Conservation Area. A casualty from earlier times is the Star Inn on the right, in existence from *c.* 1870 to around 1985.

Wentworth Street, Wakefield Girls High School

Barrister John Pemberton Heywood built the property (Wentworth House), viewed here from the Wentworth Street/Wentworth Terrace junction, between 1802 and 1803, and it remained with his wife until her death in 1851; he had died in 1835. Following the passing of the Endowed Schools Act in 1869 and the establishment of the Wakefield Grammar School Foundation in 1875, it was the latter's aim to provide a school in the city for 100 girls, leading them up to a standard for university entrance. In 1878, Wentworth House and grounds were bought from Elias Holt, a woollen manufacturer, and converted to a girls' high school at a cost of £8,000. The school has grown from fifty-nine pupils, when it first began, to approximately 750 in the present day.

Wentworth Terrace, View Looking East

The view is looking east along Wentworth Terrace to Northgate and much has happened to the stone-built Avenue House on the left, at the corner of Wentworth Street/Wentworth Terrace, during the period that separates the two pictures. Built in 1818 and containing four floors, the property became quite a celebrated art gallery between 1934–2009; is included in the Wentworth Terrace Conservation Area; and is a locally listed building. Sadly, after displaying the work of some of Britain's top artists and sculptors, it is perhaps now destined for a mundane existence, being currently offered for sale or rent. The gallery's permanent collection has been transferred to the Hepworth, which opened in 2011. The collection numbered some 5,000 works, among them being the Hepworth family gift and the rarely seen Gott collection. One of the reasons for the closure of the Wentworth Terrace gallery was the lack of space, with only around 7 per cent of the entire collection displayed at any one time. Wentworth Terrace itself contains several listed buildings, including Nos 2, 3 and 4 and St Austin's Roman Catholic church.

Wentworth Terrace, St Austin's Roman Catholic Church

Situated on the south side of Wentworth Terrace, the Roman Catholic church of St Austin was designed for the Society of Jesus by Crofton-born Joseph Ireland (*c.* 1780–1841), with modifications by mason William Puckrin. Opened on 4 March by Rt Revd Thomas Smith, a noted benefactor of the church was Thomas Waterton of Walton Hall. The red-brick building with painted sandstone dressings was altered and extended by Andrews and Delaney in 1856. A lady chapel was added under the direction of Joseph Hanson between 1878/79, and during 1930 a parish room was built. St Austin's is Grade II listed and in 2008 was amalgamated with English Martyrs church to form the Parish of St Martin de Porres.

Westgate, and the Yorkshire Penny Bank and Church Institute Buildings

The picture above dates from *c.* 1907 and shows the top of Westgate. The building occupied by the Yorkshire Penny Bank was formerly the city's first indoor corn exchange and opened in 1820. The opening up of water transport from 1702 onwards, with the development of canals crossing the Pennines, led to Wakefield becoming an important corn marketing centre. The corn exchange was built by banker Thomas Rishworth but was repossessed in 1825. To the rear was the red-brick Gothic-style Church Institute, which, along with the former corn exchange, has been demolished and the site redeveloped. The new group of buildings currently standing there are a noticeable and unfortunate omission from the impressive list of Westgate's nationally or locally listed buildings. It is also particularly disappointing when they spoil one of the city's key views noted in the Council's Upper Westgate Conservation Area report. Nonetheless, much earlier times are recalled by a blue plaque on the south side of the KoCo Bongo building that states, 'Near this site stood the public bakehouse of the lords of the manor of Wakefield. It was demolished in 1861 to make way for the Church Institute, later Youth House.'

Westgate, Bing Bada Boom

In medieval times, narrow burgage plots extended from Westgate's frontage. Then, gradually, in the eighteenth and nineteenth centuries, impressive residential properties (including magnificent Georgian town houses) fronted the plots and resulted in a street of varied architectural styles – simple Palladian and ornate Classical flavours. In later years, these buildings were turned over for use by commerce and the leisure industry. No. 61/63 on Westgate's south side was originally occupied by the White Horse coaching inn, dating back to at least 1793. Among the previous owners were Anne Lyle, Thomas Kaye, John Battison, Carters Victoria Brewery, Springwell Brewery Heckmondwike, Melbourne Brewery and Tetley's Brewery. The premises were rebuilt around the turn of the nineteenth century and have also been known as the Forehorse and Firkin. The building is currently Grade II listed. The picture above was taken in 1973, the one below in 2015, and it is a welcome sight to see the building has retained its appearance over the intervening period and not suffered any grossly inappropriate alterations. The Bing Bada Boom Facebook page states that the venue has closed its doors. Perhaps a less crazy name, more in keeping with the building's listed status, might be suggested if the premises reopens as a commercial venture once more.

Westgate, Corn Exchange/Grand Electric

A corn exchange at the top of Westgate's south side was opened in 1838, replacing an earlier one erected nearby in 1820. The new building's exterior featured Greek-style Doric columns on the ground floor and Corinthian columns above, while inside accommodation was provided for approximately 130 stands. Although enlarged in 1863/64, the building experienced dwindling trade by the turn of the nineteenth century and other uses were explored. In 1910, a cinema was housed on the first-floor saloon and ten years later, a billiard hall was established on the ground floor. Taken over by developers in 1962, the building was subsequently demolished and new commercial premises erected on the site.

Westgate End, Facing West

The top picture, facing west along Westgate End, was taken at a time when the Yorkshire (West Riding) Electric tramway's double-track lines, linking the city with Horbury and Ossett, dominated the wide road, now a busy dual carriageway. Representing the surviving western stretch of the late eighteenth-century town, much of this area now makes up the Lower Westgate Conservation Area, which was designated in 1975. Character is given to the area by the surviving sixteenth- and late eighteenth-century properties on the north side, though some, sadly, are compromised by poor quality shopfronts, signage and street furniture. This is further spoiled by unsympathetic retail developments on the road's south side, its architectural contribution in conservation terms disappointing and fragmented. The Lower Westgate Conservation report highlights several buildings of importance including Austin House at No. 160, with its large classical pediment, and the eighteenth- and nineteenth-century properties with large round-arched coach entries. Along with No. 160, Nos 136, 138 and 148 are Grade II* listed. Two smaller dwellings, dating from the early to mid-sixteenth century, Nos 162 and 166, are Grade II listed.

Westgate End, Girl at a Drinking Fountain

Taken from the Westgate End/Ings Road junction, this view is facing north. The girl not only adds marvellously to the composition, but gives some indication of scale to the granite horse trough and drinking fountain, erected to the memory of Ann Clarkson, sister of Henry Clarkson of Alverthorpe Hall. Miraculously, in spite of all demolition and redevelopment work in this stretch of properties, J. Billington's premises still survive and are currently occupied by West Gate End book shop (No. 166). Perhaps when examining the dilapidated state of James Bailey's grocery shop there is no wonder it was pulled down in later years. Nonetheless, it provides a unique glimpse at building materials formerly used to make up Wakefield's streetscape. A final comparison of the two pictures brings home that many of today's thoroughfares are spoiled by the protrusion of road furniture, yet it is refreshing to notice one of the old style telephone boxes is still extant in this area of Wakefield.

Westgate, Looking West to Westgate Tower

Looking west along Westgate, Pemberton House is visible on the right at the former entrance to Westgate railway station. The house was built around 1752 for Pemberton Milnes, member of a family of successful cloth and wine merchants. On leaving the Milnes' ownership, the property passed to author Henry Clarkson; the West Riding and Grimsby Railway; a local print works, which published *The Wakefield & West Riding Herald*; and a labour exchange. On the left, the Elephant & Castle, a survivor from the eighteenth century, is Grade II listed. Former owners have included Warwick's Ales Boroughbridge and John Smith's Brewery. A short section of the earlier railway station's brick wall is of particular interest as it features a detailed stone doorway.

Westgate Looking West, Illustrating Track Laying

The Yorkshire (West Riding) Electric Tramways Ltd's route along West Gate was double tracked. Progress on the track work may be seen in the top picture and has found a number of onlookers. The track was laid to a gauge of 4 ft 8½ inches and the roadway was excavated to a depth of 12½ inches. A bed of concrete 8 inches deep was then laid to carry the track and paving, this bed being 8 feet wide for single track and 17 feet wide for double track. Between the rails and for 18 inches on either side was paved with 5 by 4-inch granite setts. The rails comprised 6½-inch-deep girder sections with 1½ in deep grooves in which the tram wheels sat. From this point at the top of Westgate the track continued through the Bull Ring and left either north to Leeds or south through Kirkgate to Sandal or Agbrigg. Since the top picture was taken, the tram track has gone, following the introduction of motorbuses from 1932; the Yorkshire Penny Bank building on the extreme right has been demolished; and alterations of varying degrees have affected the sites and premises on Westgate's northern side.

Westgate, North Side from Carter Street, Facing East

Time has not been as kind to this section of Westgate as in other parts of the street. One of the three-storey premises has been demolished and the site infilled with a bank. In spite of this, apart from No. 76 at the Carter Street/Westgate junction, all the buildings are listed. These include Nos 72 and 74, formerly two early–mid-nineteenth century houses; No. 70 at the Cheapside corner; and the bank at No. 66. It is commendable that the signage is restrained on the listed buildings, but there is definitely a change of tenants from previous days. In the top picture, the premises of a photographer, organ seller, grocer and dyer may be identified. No. 76 was once occupied by Fred Shaw, photographer. Maybe it is him behind the camera for the top picture. But gone are the days of travelling by tram and the period when everyone stood still and watched in awe as a photographer pointed his camera at a particular scene, marvelling at the new invention. Digital cameras, phones and tablet devices have rendered taking pictures so much of a daily occurrence that nobody flinches anymore.

Westgate, Picture House

The Picture House was designed by Manchester architect Albert Winstanley under instructions from Sydney Tolfree. Built at a cost of around £13,000, it opened on 22 December 1913 and was Wakefield's first purpose-built cinema house. The building boasted a small stage and orchestra pit, along with accommodation for 1,400 patrons. In later years, the cinema operated under Essoldo and Classic Cinemas. After part of the premises was used as a skateboard centre, final closure occurred in June 1978. In subsequent years, the building has been a nightclub and pub under varying titles including Roof Top Gardens, Quest and Mustang Sally's.

Westgate Railway Station Frontage

Wakefield Westgate station was opened on 5 October 1857 by the Bradford, Wakefield & Leeds Railway, but services were operated by the GN and L&Y. The facilities moved a very short distance to the north from 1 May 1867 after the completion of the West Riding & Grimsby Railway, which offered the GN a more direct route from Doncaster to Wakefield. The station was for joint use of the GN, Midland and Manchester, Sheffield & Lincolnshire Railways. Clearly visible is the 97-foot-tall Italianate clock tower and ridge-and-furrow canopy over the platforms. The station's appearance was greatly altered during the late 1960s and included the demolition of the clock tower. However, the station is still very busy, accommodating local and intercity Leeds King's Cross trains.

Westgate Railway Station Looking North-East

Plans to reconstruct Westgate railway station, slightly north of its then existing position, were announced at the end of 2011. Costing £8.1 million, the station was unveiled at a ceremony on Sunday 22 December 2013 and included new shops, a footbridge, lifts linking the platforms, a new travel centre, first-class lounge and a standard waiting area. The entire project was a collaboration between East Coast, Network Rail, Muse Developments and Wakefield Council. East Coast said they had been aided by the quality of the design by Leeds Studio and the commitment of contractors, Buckingham Group. The company added that the new station was more energy-efficient, contained thirty sheltered bike racks and would be served by Metro's free city bus every 10 or 12 minutes. East Coast had worked alongside Wakefield Council and English Cities Fund to make sure that the station complements wider plans to regenerate the Westgate area.

Westgate South Side, Nos 67, and 75 to 83

Upper Westgate was designated a conservation area in 1975 due to its distinctive historic and architectural character. The buildings seen on the left in the modern picture (Nos 67, and 75 to 83) form an important part of it, all being Grade II listed. In total, the upper Westgate Conservation area contains twenty-seven listed buildings and thirty locally designated structures. Wakefield Council acknowledge that during the last few decades conversion of listed buildings 'has become less sympathetic to the historic environment'. However, the council presently offers guidance on shopfront design and state the removal of unsympathetic shopfronts and signage will be encouraged and control placed on new additions. The council is also pressing for a more cohesive arrangement of street furniture and instigating a more co-ordinated approach to style and siting.

Westgate, Theatre Royal and Opera House

The original theatre on this site was built by James Banks for Tate Wilkinson and opened on 7 September 1776. The premises were refused a licence for various reasons in 1892 and closed, then were demolished two years later. A new theatre, designed by Frank Matcham, opened on 15 October 1894. In 1954, the premises were converted to a cinema, becoming the Essoldo. This lasted until 1966, when the building was used for bingo. But, after extensive restoration, the premises returned to full-time theatre use from 16 March 1986.

Wood Street, Court House

Until the building of the Court House in 1810, West Riding magistrates had conducted their business in a number of local public houses. After land was obtained in 1806, prizes were offered for a suitable design for a new building and Wakefield architect Charles Watson won the competition. It has been suggested that a delay in the building work was due to the scarcity of suitable stone for the pillars. Quarter Sessions were held in the Court House upon completion in 1810. The premises were enlarged in 1849/50 and during the 1880s. Court business ceased there in 1992 and the building is Grade II listed. After standing empty for a number of years and being on English Heritage's At Risk Register, the Court House is being renovated to form an important part of the city's Civic Quarter.

Wood Street, Looking North

The vicar of St John's church between 1805 and 1825 was the Revd William Wood and Wood Street, looking north-east towards several noted buildings, was named after he, as owner of the property at the bottom, opened it up. The thoroughfare is located in a conservation area and forms an important part of the city's Civic Quarter, bordered by Wood Street itself, Bond Terrace, Rishworth Street and Northgate. Contained there are several notable listed Victorian civic buildings, an elegant terrace of Georgian buildings and a stone-fronted Edwardian public building. Over the last few years, the entire area has started to undergo a transformation. A Council Master Plan aims to regenerate the area with appropriate uses while preserving its architectural and historical character. Wood Street buildings identified in the regeneration plans to be adapted and redeveloped over the ensuing years include the old Court House, city museum and police station.

Wood Street, Town Hall

Following a competition launched to find an appropriate design for a new town hall, London architect T. E. Collcutt won the first prize of £150. Beating off stiff opposition from thirty-five other submissions, Colcutt was also the architect for London's Bloomsbury Square. Situated at the heart of Wakefield city centre, the town hall is a Grade I listed building. Still retaining many of the original Victorian features, the building is currently undergoing extensive refurbishment to make an essential contribution to the city's Civic Quarter.

Wakefield District

Agbrigg, Agbrigg Road

Agbrigg Road stretches between Barnsley Road and Doncaster Road. The top picture was taken along the thoroughfare at the junction with Belle Vue Road, extending to the left. The Duke of York public house operated as a beerhouse from around 1890 to 1897, and among the previous owners were Fernandes' Brewery and John Smith's Brewery. Tram No. 50 (built in 1905), belonging to the Yorkshire (West Riding) Electric Tramways Co. Ltd, seated fifty-six (22/34). The route to Agbrigg was opened in August 1904 and No. 50 has paused at the outer terminus, with its route indicator displaying Ossett. Agbrigg Road is currently served by motorbuses.

Belle Vue Alexandra Hotel, Doncaster Road

The Alexandra Hotel in the top picture, with J. S. Beilby shown as the landlord, can trace its history back to at least 1871, when Joseph Wade was the landlord. Among the previous owners were Fernandes' Brewery and John Smith's Brewery. The Wakefield (South) 1890 map shows the pub with only a few houses in its immediate vicinity (and along Doncaster Road), with much of Elm Tree Street, out of view to the right, still open land. Close by were a number of firms, including the Fall Ings Foundry and the City Saw Mills. The Alexandra closed in 1991 and since that time, the building has been converted for other commercial uses – initially by an auto spares company but currently for The Living Room.

Castleford Station Road

The view is looking from Bank Street towards the Picture House in Station Road. The modern picture only betrays a significant alteration on the right with the Cooperative building being swept away and replaced with a Brutalist structure. A vast change in mood and affluence may be sensed when comparing the two pictures, one taken during the 1920s and the other in 2015. Many of the men and a few boys, pictured above, presumably mostly miners, seemingly have a brooding, worried air about them. The 1920s was the time of the mining industry's slump and colliers working short time. Since the closure of the surrounding pits, Wheldale and Fryston, Castleford has struggled, yet is overcoming high unemployment and enjoying economic growth through its retail and distribution centres. Thus, in the modern picture food seems to be easily available from a number of stores, relatively new motor cars throng the streets and people walk around fashionably dressed and with a mild air of contentment.

Crofton, Cock & Crown

A remarkable scene with plenty of activity is captured in the top picture, close to the junction of Doncaster Road and Pontefract Road at Crofton. It features the Cock & Crown, which was originally called Sawyers and dated from at least 1791. The landlord is proudly posing with his wife or bar staff, along with a number of locals, horses and even a dog, outside the premises. He belongs to a time when his chosen profession offered esteem and respectability in the wider community. He was also perhaps not locked into barrelage targets from greedy brewers, or pub companies. Vaulting hurdles like that have caused many landlords to flee the trade and closed scores of pubs up and down the country. One of the most interesting sights is the dray, which is propelled by steam traction. This must belong to a particular point in time when the practice was a unique occurrence. Since then, the Cock & Crown has seemingly survived all the upheavals of the brewing industry and still presents an acceptable frontage to the road without too many assaults on the aesthete's eye. It perhaps offers a wider range of services to customers than in the previous halcyon days of the pub trade.

Hemsworth, Barnsley Road

In the top picture the pub at the Barnsley Road junction is titled the Blue Bell Hotel, with Fred Cressey as the landlord. Over the years, it has also been titled Crosshills Tavern but has since reverted back to the Blue Bell. Noticeable too, in the modern picture, is the conversion of one half of the pub (on the right) to a ladies' hairdressing salon. This section in the past has also accommodated a pets and aquatics store. The Blue Bell is one of many pubs that has downsized in a once buoyant, but now increasingly shrinking, market. At the end of 2014, it was estimated that thirty-one British pubs were closing per week. The peak closure period was between January and June 2009 when fifty-two pubs ceased trading every week. Hemsworth, on the edge of West Yorkshire, was once heavily reliant on coal mining though the closure of the pits during the 1980s led to deprivation, high crime rates and unemployment, the small town being in the top 2 per cent of deprived areas in the whole EU. Thankfully, Hemsworth, along with neighbouring villages, was made into a special regeneration area, and fortunes have improved as a result.

Horbury, Queen Street

A noted change to occur here over time has been the close attention to security by the stores depicted during out of trading hours. The bottom picture was taken on a Sunday afternoon when the jeweller's window was notably cleared of items, a sign on the window announcing to would-be thieves during trading hours that the premises were fitted with 'Fog Bandit' – a high-speed security fogging system. On either side of the jeweller's, two shops have roller shuttering protecting windows and doors. Sadly, while being unsightly, this type of security is necessary today. At the time of the old picture, Horbury, which included the outlying areas of Horbury Bridge and Horbury Junction, had relied for many years on old industries such as woollens (at the Albion Mills and Millfield Mills), engineering (at Richard Sutcliffe's Universal Works) and railway wagon building (at Charles Roberts & Co's works). As these declined, Horbury became a largely residential area. Along with the jeweller's, there are other high-class clothes, food, bookshops and cafés situated in the vicinity; some are even local family owned and run, giving the town strong individuality.

Normanton High Street

The main changes to occur in this section of Normanton High Street have involved the two of the three buildings that once added character to the area. They are the swimming baths and Majestic cinema (operated by Star Cinemas from 1936 and closed in 1964), visible to the right in the top picture. Peculiarly, both sites were taken recently by one developer (Asda supermarkets) and merged into a single new development. With some alterations to its frontage, the old baths structure presently houses an Asda store, while the former Majestic was demolished and the site cleared to facilitate room for an adjacent car park. Old Victorian/Edwardian swimming baths and Art Deco cinema buildings have been demolished in great numbers throughout the country. The one great advantage in this location – even though only one former building has survived in part – is that the new development has found employment for a small number of people living in an area of West Yorkshire, where it is greatly needed. On the street's opposite side, the Baptist chapel, built in 1877, continues to thrive. But it too has experienced misfortune as, during 2009, arsonists set it ablaze. The building was restored to its former glory in 2013.

Normanton Market Place Tram Terminus

On Monday 29 October 1906, the Yorkshire (West Riding) Electric Tramways Ltd opened a 'detached tramway' (one that did not link with Wakefield) from Normanton through Castleford to Pontefract. Prior to the opening of the route, a number of trams from the Wakefield system to serve the new route were taken on low loaders, hauled by steam traction engines, from Rothwell Haigh Depot to one at Castleford. Above, West Riding car No. 30 is at the Normanton terminus on the end of High Street and close to the Market Place. The company's last vehicle ran on the above mentioned route on Sunday 1 November 1925. Normanton is south-east from Wakefield and during the nineteenth century was an important railway town. Later, it enjoyed a boom period, being served by a number of collieries (Don Pedro and St John's) and several brickworks. By the mid-1970s, most of the Normanton area coal seams were redundant, causing the town to suffer decline, especially after the 1984/85 Miners' Strike. The bottom picture shows quite a number of buildings have been demolished and new ones added in the Market Place, yet the area still forms a focal point for the town, albeit in a reduced way. This is because over the last few decades, the town has grown as a commuter suburb of the Leeds City area.

Ossett, and Tram Terminus

In the top picture, taken *c.* 1904, looking towards the top of Dale Street, a Yorkshire (West Riding) Electric tram has just arrived in Bank Street, Ossett, and is parked at the terminus. It was working the company's passenger service from Agbrigg to Ossett, via Wakefield and Horbury, a route opened on 15 August 1904. On the left is the London City and Midland Bank. Immediately to the right of the tram is the grammar school, built in 1834 to replace an older structure; it was in turn demolished for the construction of the town hall, formally opened on 2 June 1908. It was designed by A. W. Hanstock of Batley, cost £23,000 to build and is Grade II listed. In the same year, the tram terminus was moved to the top of Dale Street. The Pickard Fountain, along with troughs for horses and dogs, is to the right, provided in 1893 by Miss Hannah Pickard, a member of an Ossett textile family. Designed by W. A. Kendall, it was relocated to Green Park during the 1980s but has since been removed. The Perserverence Mill chimney is evident on the right. Currently, the entire area depicted forms part of the Ossett Conservation Area and is pedestrianised.

Outwood Empire

Opened in 1921, Outwood's Empire Cinema was owned and operated by Rothwell Empire Ltd, with seating for 750 patrons. It was built, as were numbers of other suburban cinemas, once the building restrictions were lifted after the First World War. Showing one feature nightly, the cinema's admission prices ranged between 4*d* and 10*d* per person. The proscenium was 27 feet wide, though on the installation of CinemaScope was widened to 35 feet. At the front of the building was a fish-and-chip shop and a DIY store. After closure as a cinema in 1964, the building opened as a bingo hall around three years later and this lasted until 1987. Thereafter, the premises were used as a nursery and a carpet store but in 1995 were opened as the UK's first drive-through fish-and-chip takeaway, which also incorporated a 'themed' restaurant. The movie-themed restaurant was much discussed when it first opened and even featured on the *Big Breakfast* show for the largest amount of fish and chips served in an hour.

Outwood, Leeds Road

Double-deck, top-covered, open balcony car No. 39 belonging to the Yorkshire (West Riding) Electric Tramways is in Leeds Road at Outwood while travelling, in a northerly direction, to Leeds. The availability of cheap transport fostered housing and other developments along Leeds Road. Many of the buildings (mostly residential on the left) have been greatly altered, some for commercial purposes, while the Queen Hotel in existence from at least 1871 and built by William Teasdale, is much enlarged. Once a small pit village, Outwood has seen much new housing building over the last twenty-five years that it is presently a greatly transformed area.

Pontefract Market Place

Once the commercial centre of the medieval town of Pontefract, the market area has been developing from the twelfth century onwards. In 1484, Pontefract was granted a charter by Richard III, giving the right to a Saturday market every week forever and two town fairs for six days. The Buttercross, seen on the right, was erected in 1734, while St Giles church, looking on to the Market Place, was originally built at the beginning of the twelfth century as a chapel of ease to the parish church of All Saints. In the mid-seventeenth century, when All Saints suffered extensive damage during the Civil War, St Giles emerged as the new parish church, a new tower being added in 1707. The Pontefract Market Place Conservation Area Appraisal and Management Plan, adopted during 2010, states that Market Place itself has a largely consistent architectural style 'which is a key aspect of its character'. It is also mentioned that No. 26, a late nineteenth-century building on the extreme right, with its gabled dormers and turret, stands as an imposing landmark. The building on the left, however, despite having the historical scale of much of the area, arguably lacks architectural quality.

Sandal, The Castle Inn

The Castle Inn was formerly titled the Cross Keys and held the title between 1785 and 1822. John Schorsey was the landlord between 1785 and 1811. Brewers once associated with the premises have included the Tadcaster Tower Brewery and Bass Brewery. Looking north in the Wakefield direction, there have been few structural changes to the premises since the time of the top picture apart from the extension at the side, which blends quite satisfactorily with the rest of the building. Trams operated by the Yorkshire (West Riding) Electric Tramways ran from Thwaite Gate to Sandal and the outer terminus of the latter was near to the Castle Inn.

Stanley, West Riding Lunatic Asylum

Following the County Asylums Act of 1808, county asylums could be established for the care and treatment of the insane poor. Thus, the West Riding Pauper Lunatic Asylum at Wakefield was built by the West Riding Magistrates, as it was their responsibility to care for the lunatic poor. The asylum (later named Stanley Royd hospital) was constructed by local builders, north-east of the city centre, at a cost of £23,000. Set in an area of 25 acres, it was occupied by 1818. During the late nineteenth century, the hospital was treating over 1,500 patients and was practically self contained, having its own farm, brewery, chapel, bookbinders and in-house fire-fighting service. The institution finally closed its doors in 1995 and some of the original buildings have since been converted to flats.

South Elmsall, Barnsley Road

The small town of South Elmsall is one of Wakefield's most southern districts being only approximately 1 mile from the Doncaster, South Yorkshire border. The area underwent a vast transformation, enjoyed regular employment and a buoyant economy when the nearby Frickley Colliery was sunk during the early years of the twentieth century. Doncaster photographer Edgar Leonard Scrivens made a habit of photographing colliery developments in a number of Yorkshire areas, and Barnsley Road is shown facing west, towards the Market Place and the Plough public house. When Scrivens was here, doubtless the commercial premises along Barnsley Road catered for most of the community's needs. Since the colliery closed towards the end of 1993, it has witnessed much hardship. The establishment of the nearby Dale Lane industrial estate, containing a number of colossal distribution warehouses of many common high street names, has been one of the key expansion areas and gone some way to give a little hope for the town's economy, and Barnsley Road.

Walton Hall

Built in the Classical style around 1768, Walton Hall's most noted occupant was eccentric taxidermist and naturalist Charles Waterton (1782–1865). During the 1820s, Charles built a 9-foot-high wall around 3 miles (5 km) of the estate, turning it into the world's first wildfowl and nature reserve. This made him one of the western world's first environmentalists. Inside, Walton Hall was crowded with natural history items, Charles' taxidermal creations, strange mementoes from his trips abroad and classical paintings. Following his death, Charles' only heir, Edmund, sold Walton Hall to family enemies, the Simpsons, in 1877. Existing on an island and accessed only by a pedestrian bridge, the Hall presently forms the main building of a hotel.

Wrenthorpe, Silcoates School

The first school dates back to 1820 when it was founded by a number of Congregationalists. Opening in Silcoates Hall, it closed not long afterwards. Succeeded by a grammar school and commercial academy, this also failed. However, a third venture was more successful, and in 1871, an enlarged school opened at Silcoates after the governors purchased the premises for £15,000. Sadly, the building was almost completely gutted by fire on 13 April 1904. Undeterred, those involved with running the establishment decided to continue and rebuild the premises. Until that occurred, the school was temporarily housed in a hotel in Harrogate and a house in Saltburn. Silcoates reopened in 1908 and over the years has enjoyed high standards in academic achievement, which continue today.